Really Cool Animal Poems

Linda Taylor

REALLY COOL ANIMAL POEMS

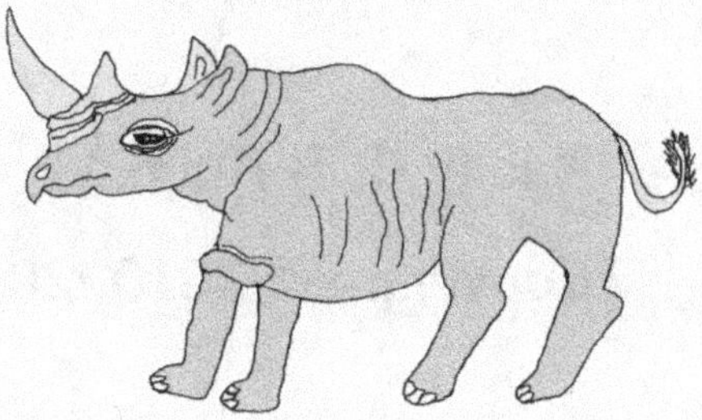

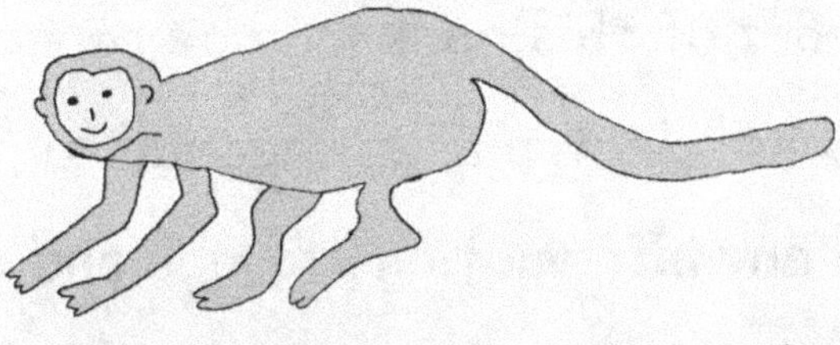

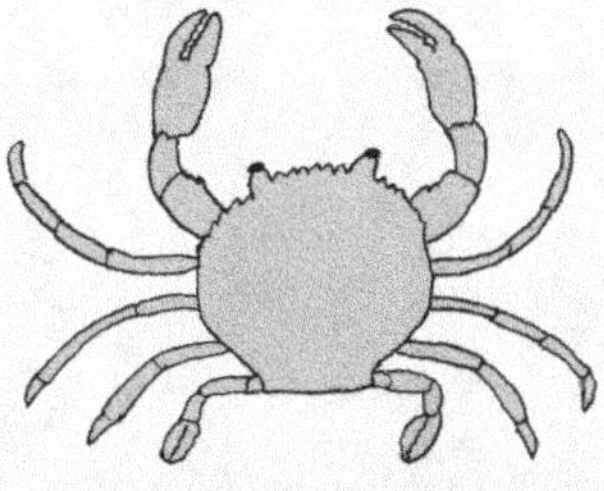

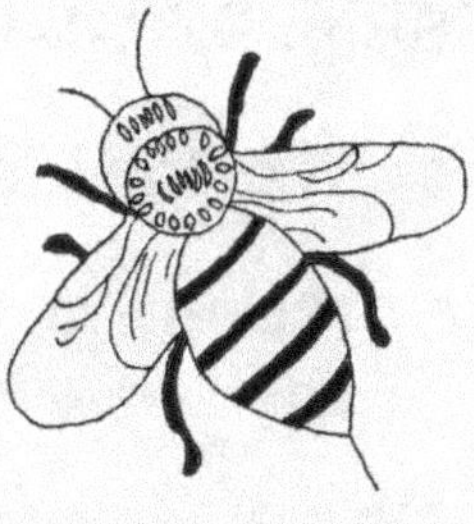

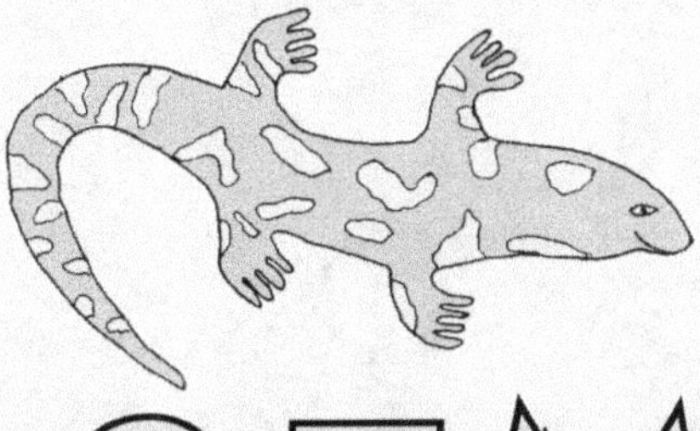

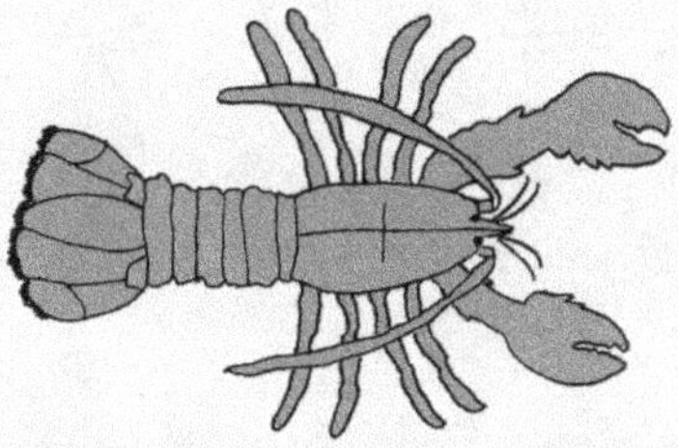

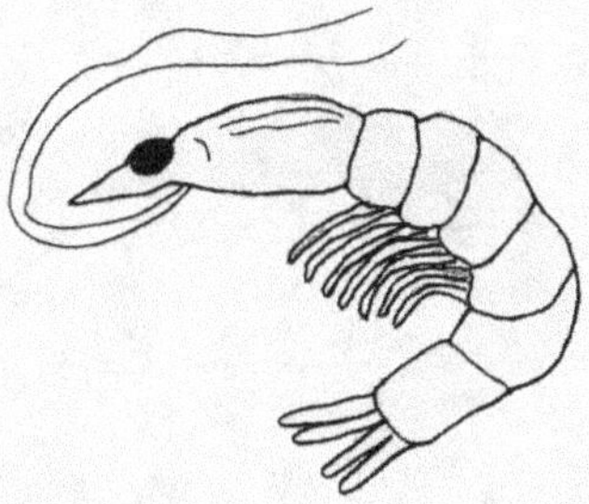

A Fun, Learning Experience for All Students

Written and Illustrated by
Linda Taylor

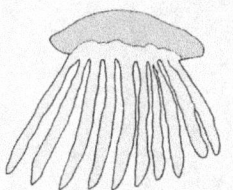

Really Cool Animal Poems Written and Illustrated by Linda Taylor
Copyright ©2010, 2019 Linda Taylor

All rights reserved. No part of this book may be reproduced or transmitted in any form or by any means, electronic or mechanical, including photo-copying, recording, or by any information storage and retrieval system without permission in writing from the copyright owner.

ISBN: 978-1-947829-91-6
For Worldwide Distribution
Printed in the U.S.A.

Touch Point Productions & Publishing
Long Island, NY

Please visit our website: diane-divine.com

To animal lovers everywhere.

—L.T.

CONTENTS

REALLY COOL ANIMALS 1

AMPHIBIANS 3
Frog 4
Salamander 5

ARACHNIDS 7
Scorpion 8
Spider 9

BIRDS 11
Chicken 12
Duck 13
Eagle 14
Flamingo 15
Ostrich 16
Owl 17
Penguin 18
Turkey 19
Woodpecker 20

COELENTERATES (GRABBY ARMS) 21
Coral 22
Jellyfish 23
Sea Anemone 24

CRUSTACEANS (SHELLIES) 25
Crab 26
Lobster 27
Shrimp 28

ECHINODERMS (CREEPERS) 29
Sand Dollar 30
Sea Urchin 31
Starfish 32

FISH 33
Catfish 34
Electric Eel 35
Seahorse 36
Shark 37

INSECTS 39
Ant 40
Bumblebee 41
Butterfly 42
Ladybug 43

MAMMALS 45
Bear 46
Beaver 47
Camel 48
Cat 49

Cheetah	50
Cow	51
Deer	52
Dog	53
Donkey	54
Elephant	55
Fox	56
Giraffe	57
Goat	58
Hippopotamus	59
Horse	60
Lion	61
Monkey	62
Pig	63
Platypus	64
Porcupine	65
Otter	66
Rabbit	67
Rhinoceros	68
Sheep	69
Squirrel	70
Tiger	71
Whale	72
Zebra	73

MARSUPIALS ... 75
Kangaroo ... 76
Koala ... 77
Opossum ... 78

MOLLUSKS (SOFTIES) ... 79
Octopus ... 80
Snail ... 81
Squid ... 82

REPTILES ... 83
Alligator ... 84
Dinosaur ... 85
Lizard ... 86
Snake ... 87
Turtle ... 88

ANIMALS ON THE MOVE ... 89
Camouflage ... 90
Habitats ... 91
Hibernation ... 92
Migration ... 93
Nocturnal Animals ... 94

REALLY COOL ANIMALS

Really cool animals
Interesting beings.
Some cuddly,
some funny,
and some I wouldn't like seeing.

Some fast
and some slow.
Some above ground
and some below.

Predators and prey.
In different environments they stay.
Unique in their ways.
I love the animal craze!

AMPHIBIANS

Amphibians are found all over the world
in places that are warm and wet.
They live partly on land and partly in water.
A frog would make a very good pet.
Ribbit, ribbit.

Frog

From eggs to tadpoles
to full grown frogs.
They love the pond and moist places
maybe near a log.

They carry their eggs in many places:
in their mouth, stomach, or pouch on their back.
Frogs are amphibians,
and those are the froggy facts.

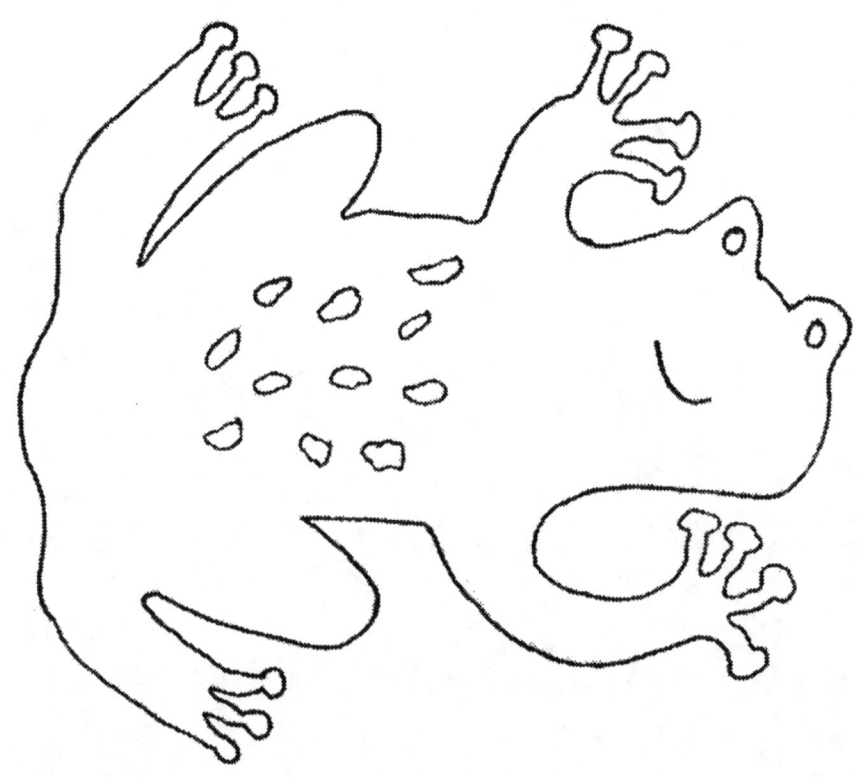

Salamander

They have rubbery bodies
and a long, long tail.
They eat worms and insects,
slugs and snails.

Some have poisonous skin
so don't go near.
Although they're bright and colorful,
we should still steer clear.

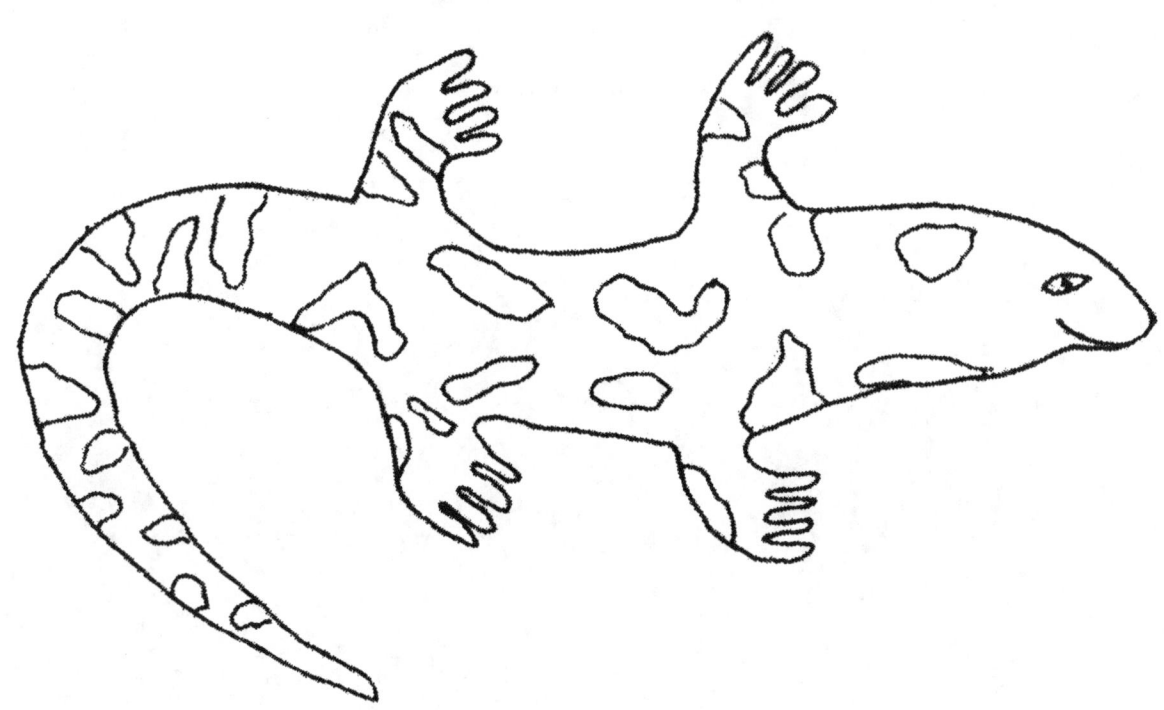

ARACHNIDS

Arachnids have eight legs,
and mostly live on land.
Spiders are the most popular ones.
Scorpions are mostly near sand.

Ticks and mites are so tiny
that you can barely seem them at all.
You might even need a microscope
if you want to see them crawl.

I DON'T WANT TO SEE THEM AT ALL!

Scorpion

Scorpions are terribly feared,
and their tail is the reason why.
It produces a powerful sting
that can paralyze any passerby.

Their body is somewhat flattened,
and they have two powerful pincers too.
They eat other insects and spiders,
I've only seen a few.
How about you?

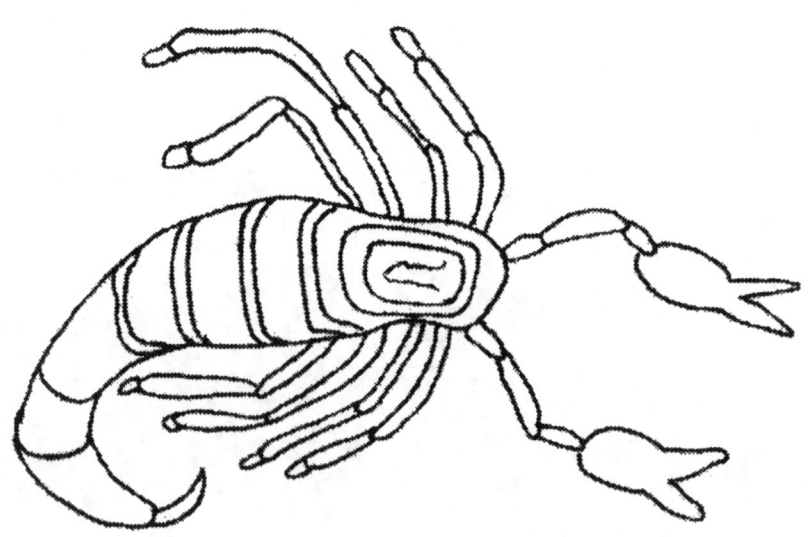

Spider

Eight-legged creatures
with two body parts.
They can spin a web and catch a bug.
That's really very smart.

They always catch their prey
in a most peculiar way.
Some are very poisonous,
and some just like to play.

BIRDS

Birds have feathers,
And birds have wings.
They have beaks or bills,
And some can even sing.

Most birds fly,
but some cannot.
Birds lay eggs
and flock together a lot.

Chicken

Some chickens lay eggs
that people love to eat.
Some can fly just a little.
It's a very popular meat.

The baby is called a chick.
The mommy is called a hen.
The daddy is called a rooster.
But they're all chickens!

Duck

Quack, quack! Honk, honk!
They make very interesting sounds.
They have webbed feet
and like to follow each other around.

Their babies are called ducklings.
The feathered winged birds do fly.
My favorite is the mallard.
They flock together in the sky.

Eagle

A strong heavy bird,
a bird of prey.
They feed on small animals
they hunt every day.

They have great talons
and a hooked beak too.
The bald eagle is a respected bird,
A symbol of justice tried and true.

Flamingo

They have bright pink feathers
and an S-shaped neck.
Their legs look like stilts.
They scoop food from the water, not peck.
They eat shrimp, snails, and algae.

On their mound of mud, they nest.
They lay one egg at a time.
They live in warm habitats,
which are the best.

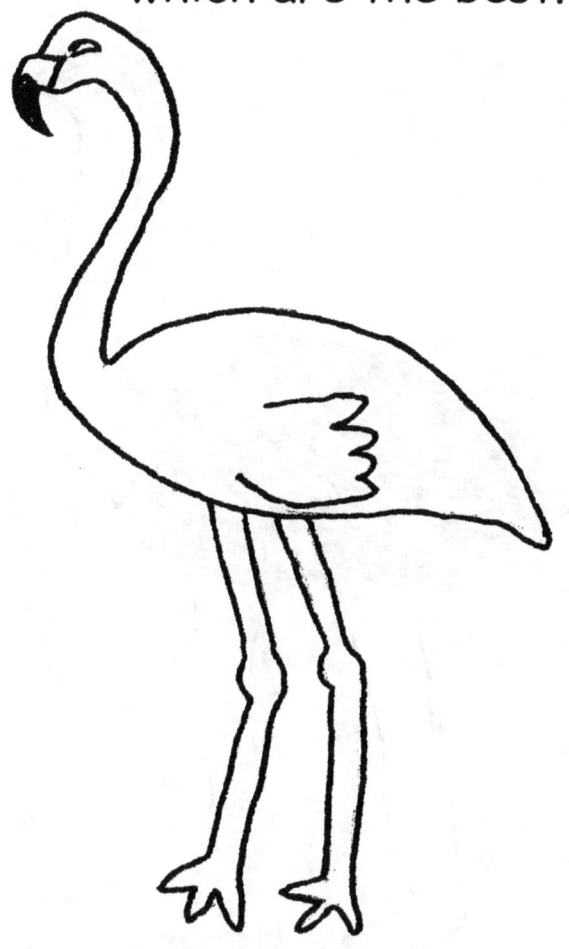

Ostrich

The tallest bird in the world,
it has a really long neck
with black and white feathers.
They hunt for food and peck.

Too big to fly,
they can run really fast.
If they were in a race,
they would not come in last.

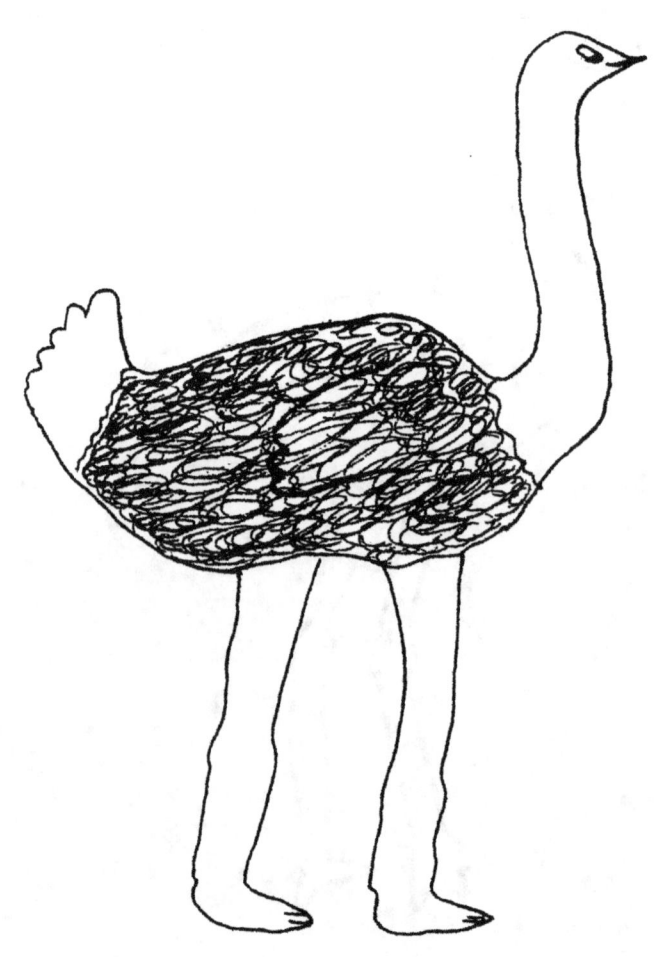

Owl

Owls go WHOOO
as they perch on a tree.
They're nocturnal animals
as we can see.

They can't really move or roll their eyes,
so they have extra movement in their neck.
Some can turn almost 270 degrees.
They love to hunt and peck.

Penguin

Penguins have black and white feathers
but cannot fly.
They make a quacking sound
as they waddle on by.

They look like they're wearing tuxedos.
All they're missing is the bow.
They slip and slide on snow and ice,
and they're excellent swimmers, you know.

Turkey

A turkey is a heavy bird.
It has a red wattle called a snood.
They only fly for short distances,
but they can run really fast when pursued.

A turkey can strut with their feathers on a farm.
A very proud bird, I'd say.
What I like best about turkeys
is that they make a great dinner
on Thanksgiving Day!

Woodpecker

Woodpecker, woodpecker,
pecking at trees.
They make so many holes
and do this with ease.

Looking for ants
and termites to eat,
They peck, peck away
until their search is complete.

COELENTERATES
(AKA GRABBY ARMS)

There are various groups of sea creatures
that live in the water as well.
One group is called coelenterates (AKA Grabby Arms).
There's really a lot to tell.

Simple creatures with hollow bodies,
They have tentacles to help catch food.
Some of them have poisonous, stinging hairs
and use them when they're in the mood.

Coral

It has a stumpy, short body around its mouth
and tentacles that sting.
As the tentacles trail in the water,
little fish really love to cling.

It builds a hard case for protection.
As years pass, it will become a coral reef.
It can grow so big and beautiful,
that some look in disbelief.

Jellyfish

It looks like a floating umbrella
filled with lots of jelly.
Not the kind you eat with peanut butter
or find at the deli.

They can be very colorful
with their tentacles hanging down.
But they're poisonous and can give a sting
if they see any enemies around.

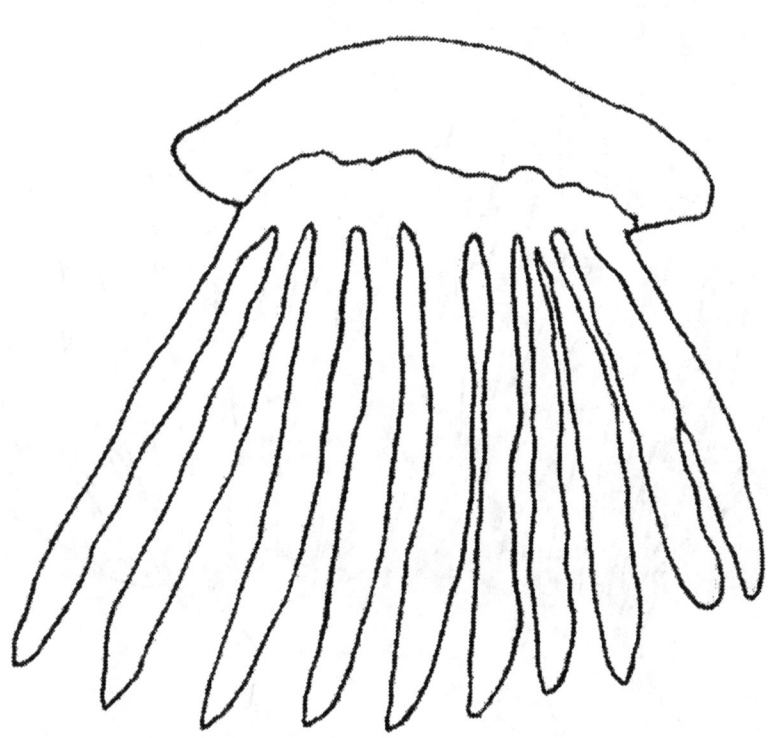

Sea Anemone

Sea anemones are such a great wonder.
They look majestic on the ocean floor.
But if fish get too close to them
and they're hungry, they will devour.

They also have stinging tentacles
they gently wave to and fro.
They use their suckers to stick on rocks,
and they usually lay really low.
Watch your step wherever you go.

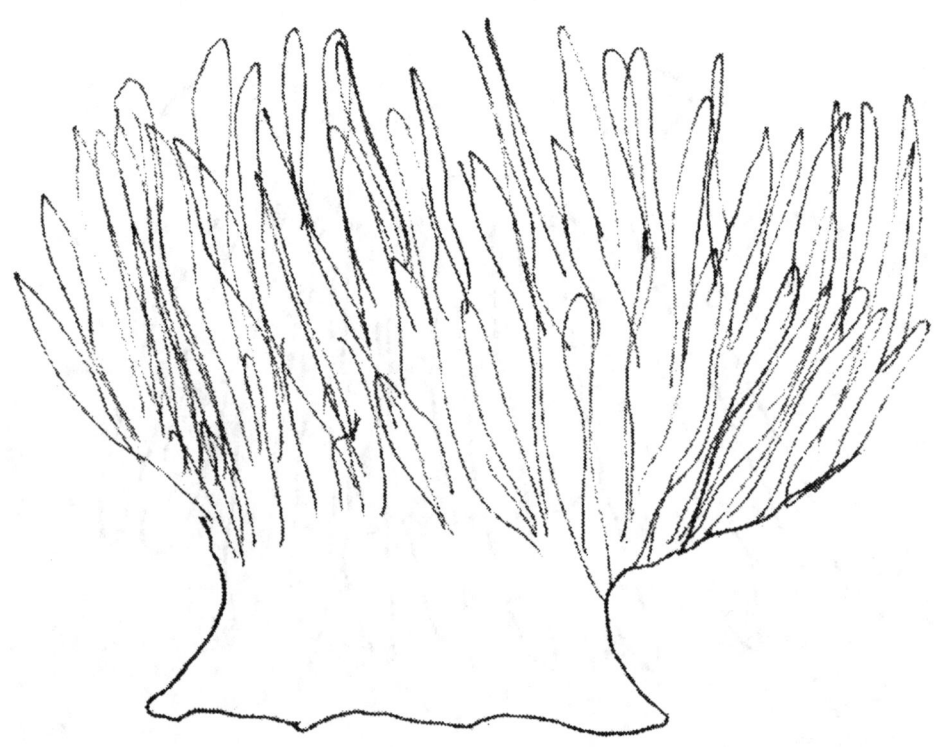

CRUSTACEANS
(AKA SHELLIES)

There's a unique group of sea creatures
that all live in a shell.
They are called crustaceans, AKA shellies,
that seafood farmers love to sell.

They have hard outer shells with many legs.
In the water is where they stay.
Some are closely related to insects.
They are very similar in some ways.

Many crustaceans are farmed for humans to eat.
Seafood, they are so named.
This food is quite delicious to taste,
I really must proclaim!

Crab

Crabs are super duper old.
They were around many, many years ago.
There are thousands of species.
Some can live on land and in oceans below.

They have ten legs, including a pair of claws,
which they use to catch their prey.
For dinner, crabs are boiled or baked
and served on my dinner tray.

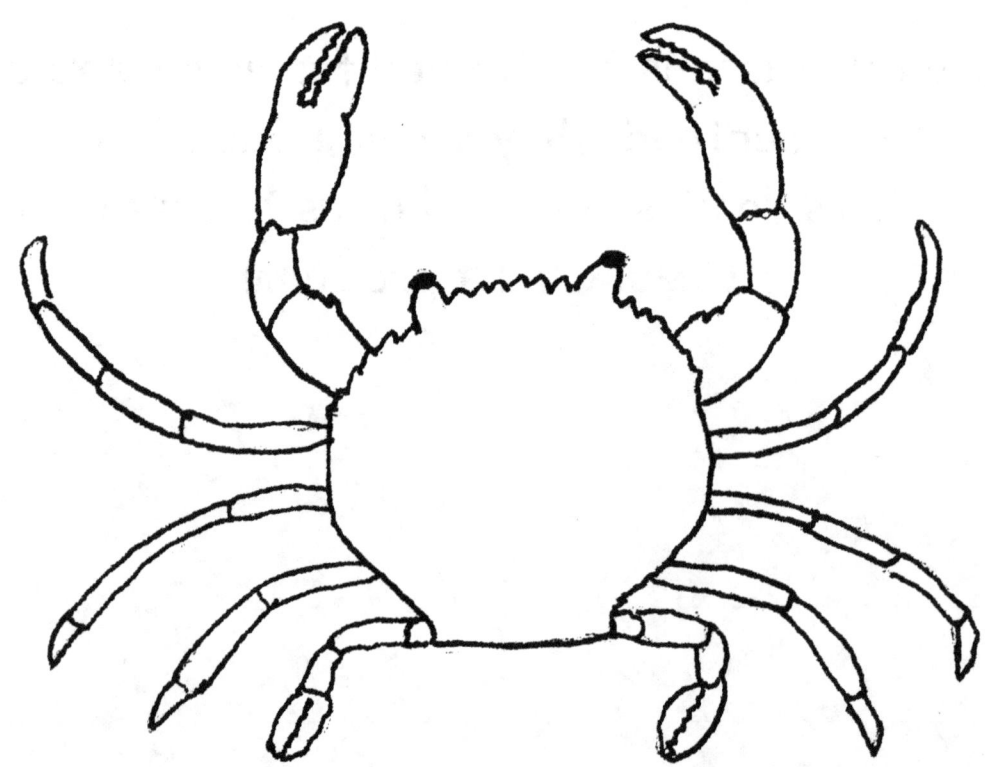

Lobster

Lobsters have long bodies with muscular tails
and live on the ocean floor.
If you had one taste of this delicious creature,
you would definitely ask for more.

A healthy source of protein,
with vitamins and minerals too.
They are only red when they're cooked.
In nature they can be green, yellow, or blue.
They are very expensive too.

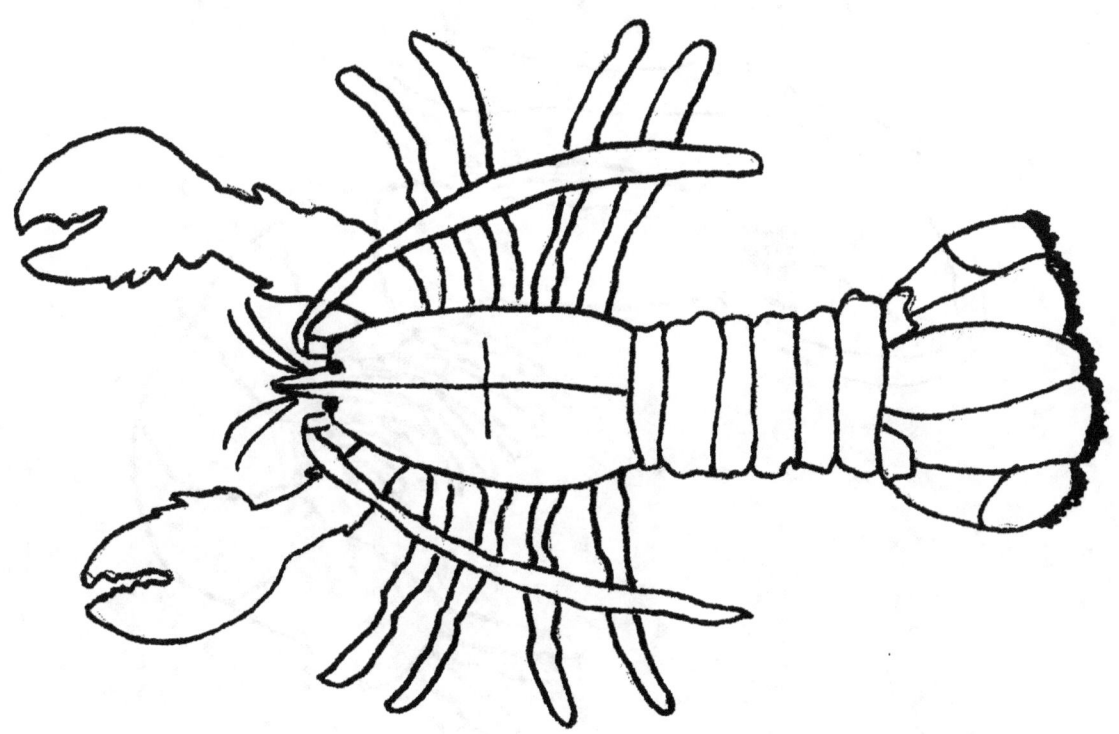

Shrimp

Thousands of shrimp species live around the world.
They come in different sizes.
They don't live long, and they aren't so strong,
But they are easy to visualize.

Many sea creatures depend on them.
They are a major meal.
They certainly look great
on my dinner plate.
A shrimp dinner is ideal.

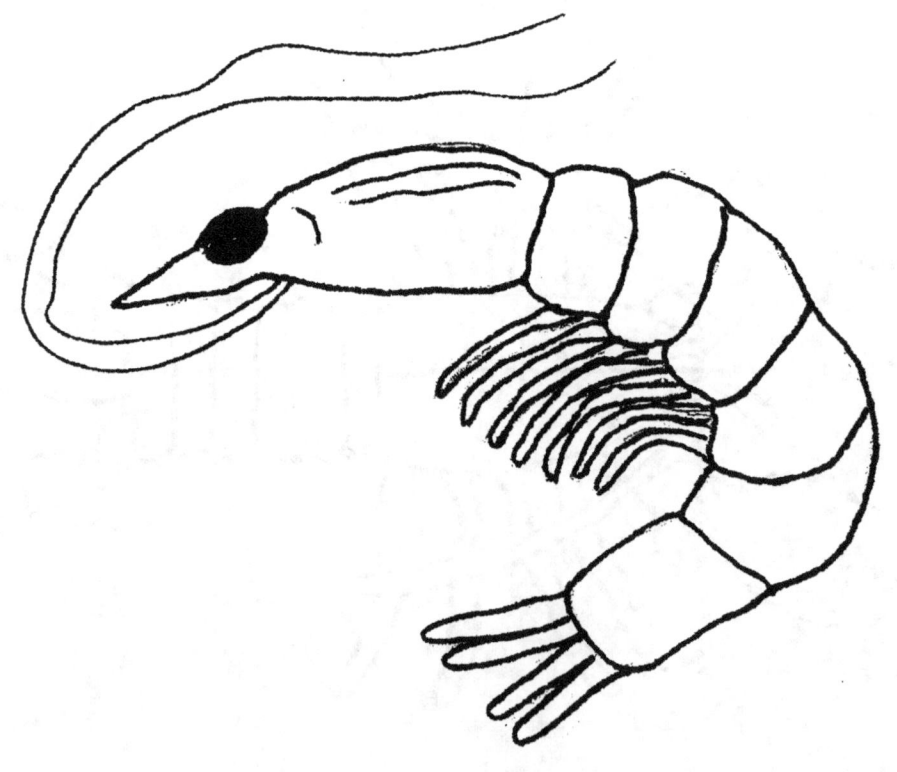

ECHINODERMS
(AKA CREEPERS)

There's a special group of sea creatures
that really have an interesting name.
They are called echinoderms (AKA Creepers).
They have qualities that are the same.

Their outer body is covered with small, hard plates,
and they move about with hundreds of small feet.
These tube feet have suction pads
that stick to things so they can creep.

Sand Dollar

Most people know that a sand dollar
is not real money, you see.
It probably got its name since it looks like a coin
and is also yellow like sand in the sea.

It's mostly in shallow waters
and sea beds all around.
It really doesn't move much
but stays mostly on the ground.

Sea Urchin

Little round sea urchins.
You'll find them on the ocean ground.
Most of the time you'll see them,
they're relatively small and round.

They have brittle spines on the outside
and feed on tiny plants in the sea.
They also feed on small animals
but NOT the sea anemone.

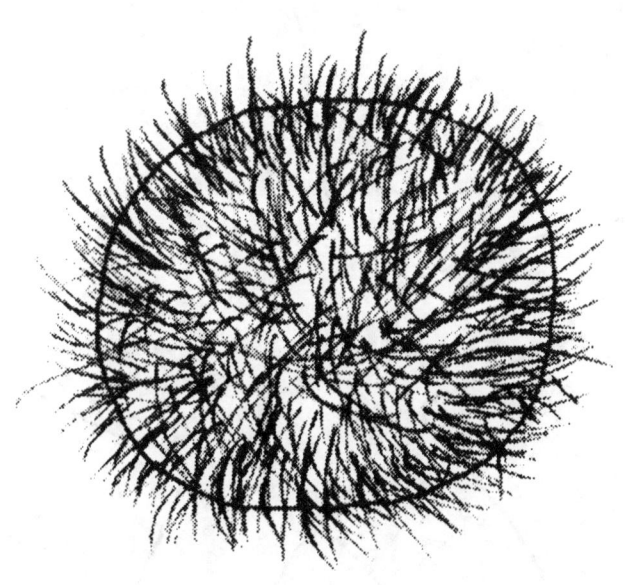

Starfish

They come in many different sizes
and many different colors as well.
Their arms can grab and hold you.
Sometimes they lay next to a shell.

They have five long arms with suckers to hold on
and crawl along the bottom of the sea.
If they get into a scuffle and lose an arm,
another grows back, I guarantee.

FISH

Fish have fins,
and they have scales.
Their gills help them breathe.
A fish is not a whale.

They come in many different
shapes and sizes.
Some are bright and colorful.
I can't believe my eyes.

Catfish

It looks like a cat
with long whiskers on its face.
They help to find the food it needs
as it swims around the place.

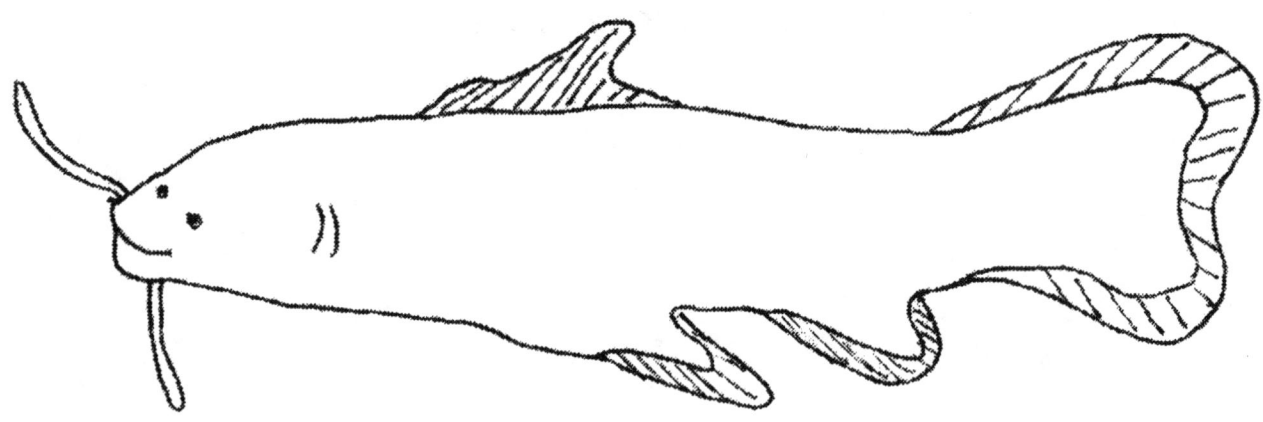

Electric Eel

A very unique fish, the only one of its kind.
Electric eels aren't really eels at all.
They're part of the knife fish family.
That's just what they're called.

They have about 6000 cells that produce
electricity to give their prey a shock.
Mostly blind, they use a radar type system.
They are air breathers and don't like to flock.

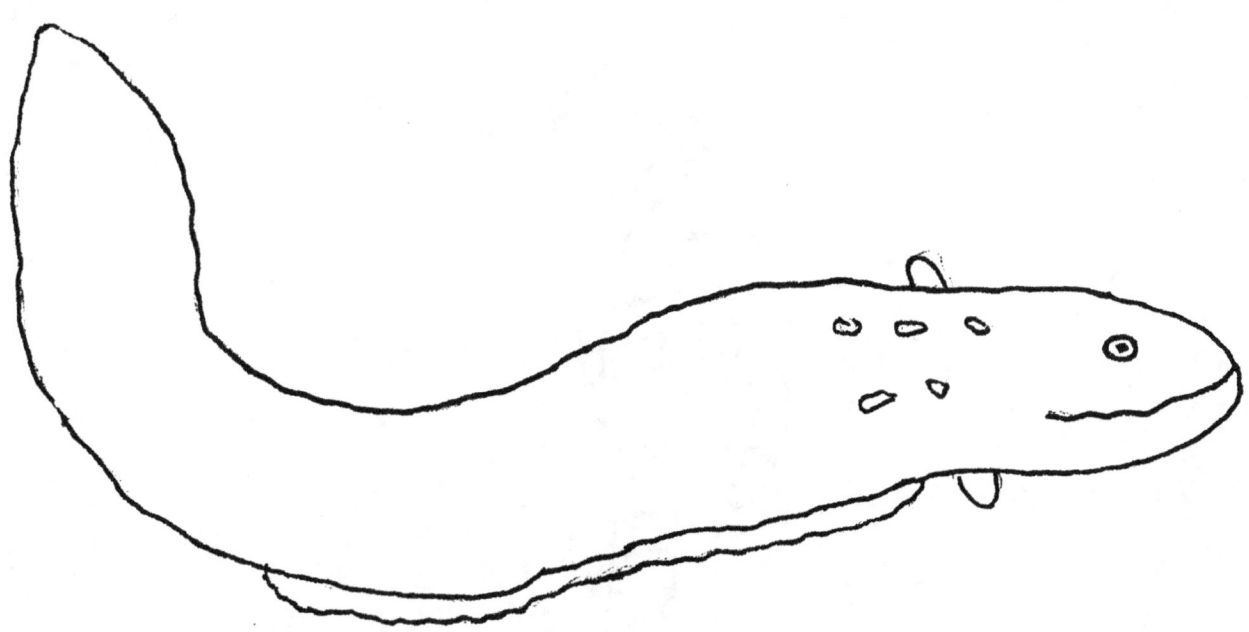

Seahorse

A small sea creature
with the head of a horse.
It moves slowly in the water,
flipping its fins of course.

It has the tail of a monkey
and a pouch like a kangaroo.
Mommy lays her eggs in Daddy's pouch.
He also gives birth too.
What an unusual thing to do!

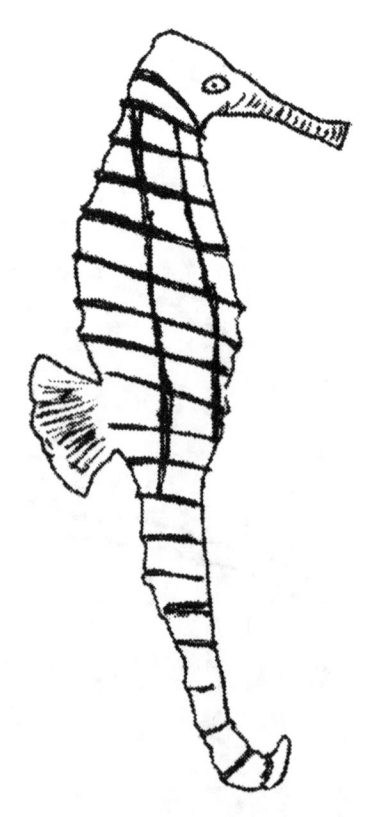

Shark

A shark is a fish
I wouldn't want to meet.
Whenever a tooth falls out of its mouth,
it grows brand new teeth.

It can be very dangerous
and is feared by many in the sea.
When it swims in sight
in the day or night,
many other sea creatures flee.
If they could talk, they'd say,
"Please don't eat me!"

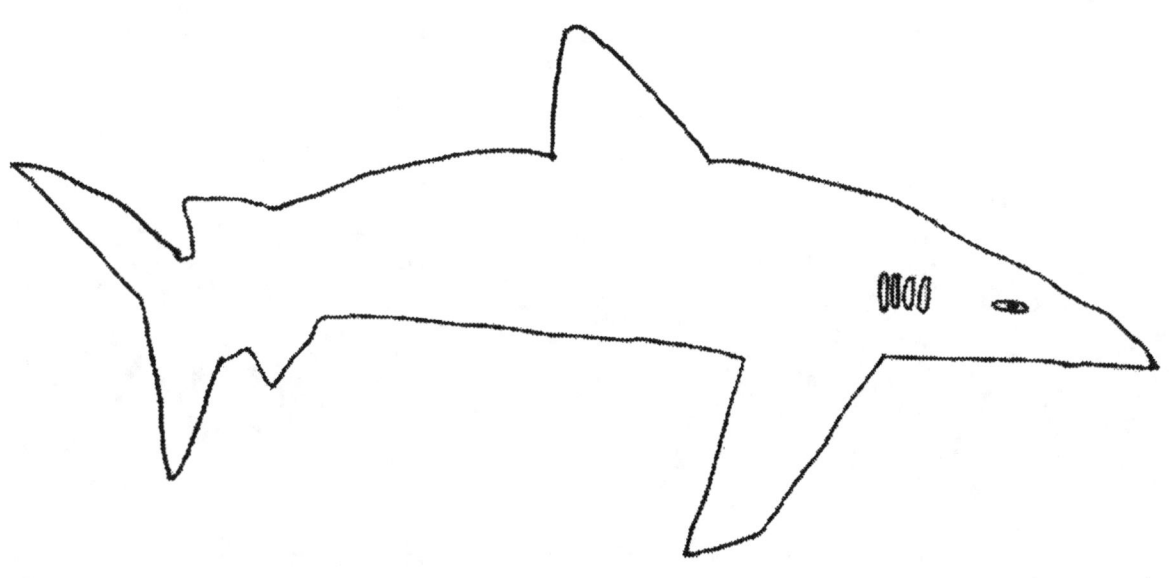

INSECTS

The three parts of an insect,
Shall I begin?
They are the head, the thorax,
and the abdomen.

They have six jointed legs,
and most have wings.
Sometimes I shoo them away
to avoid an awful sting.

Ant

Ants crawl around,
usually many together.
We don't see them too much
in inclement weather.

They're really hard workers,
and they build anthills.
They also love a picnic lunch
and lots of sticky spills.

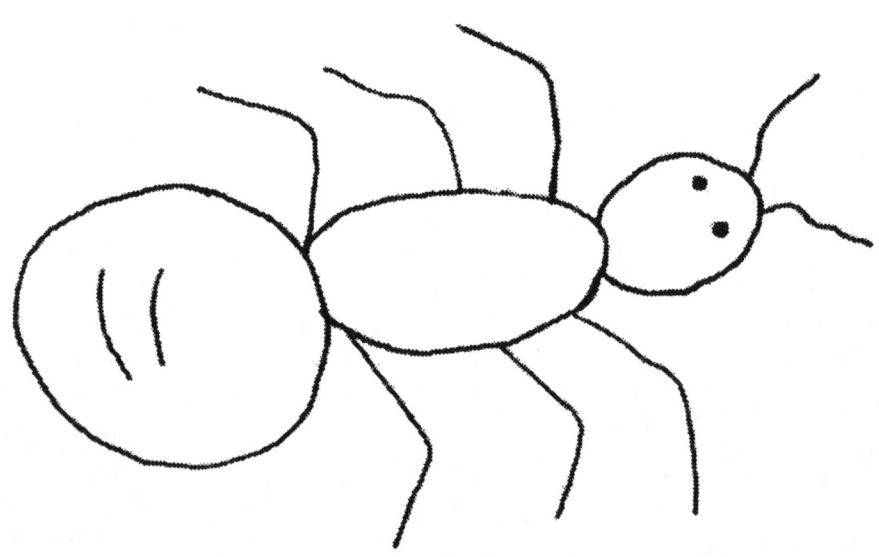

Bumblebee

Bumblebee, bumblebee
I sure hope you don't sting me.
Sipping nectar from the flower,
Giving nature lots of power.

We need you
to do your task.
But don't sting me,
just buzz on past.

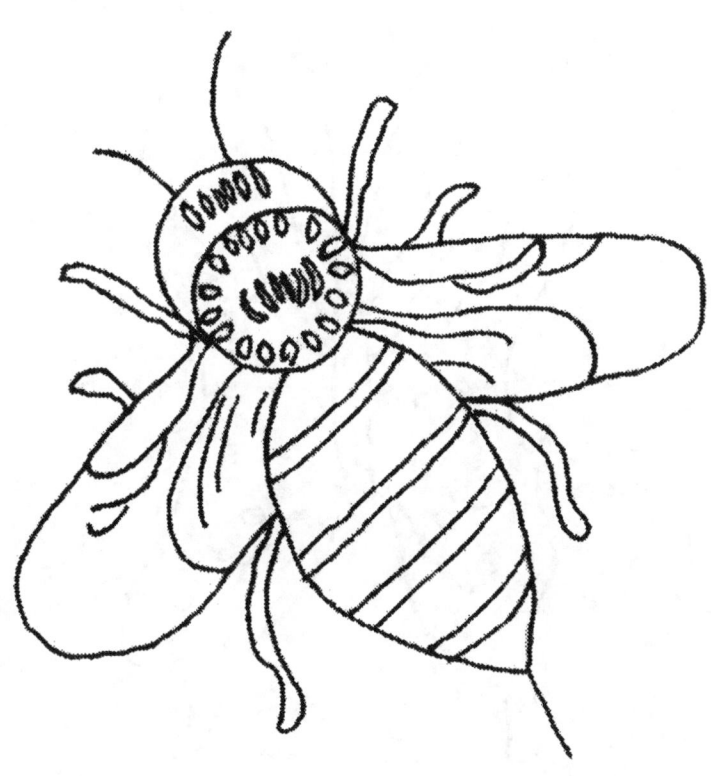

Butterfly

Butterflies, butterflies
flitter and flutter around.
Showing bright colors
as they fly up and down.

First you were a caterpillar,
Then you slept in a cocoon.
Now you are so beautiful,
Just like a flower, you've bloomed.

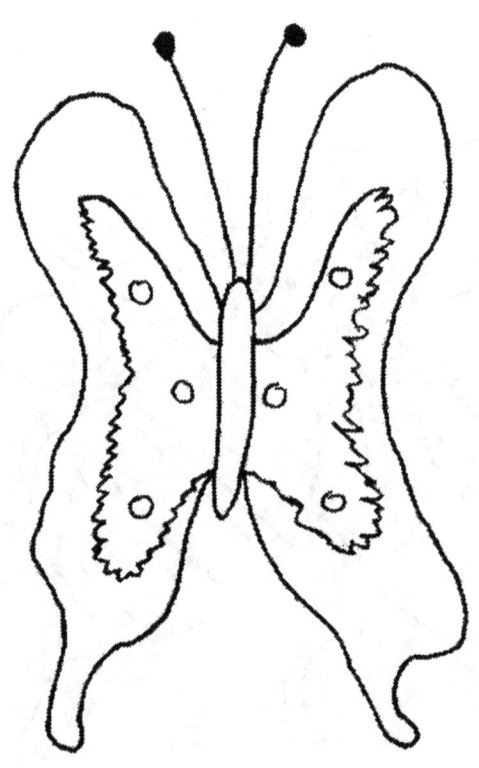

Ladybug

A brightly colored beetle,
They have thick wings that form a case.
I see them crawling all around,
but they also fly all over the place.

They can have different patterns of spots
on different colored backgrounds.
They're very useful in gardens,
for they eat aphids that can be found.

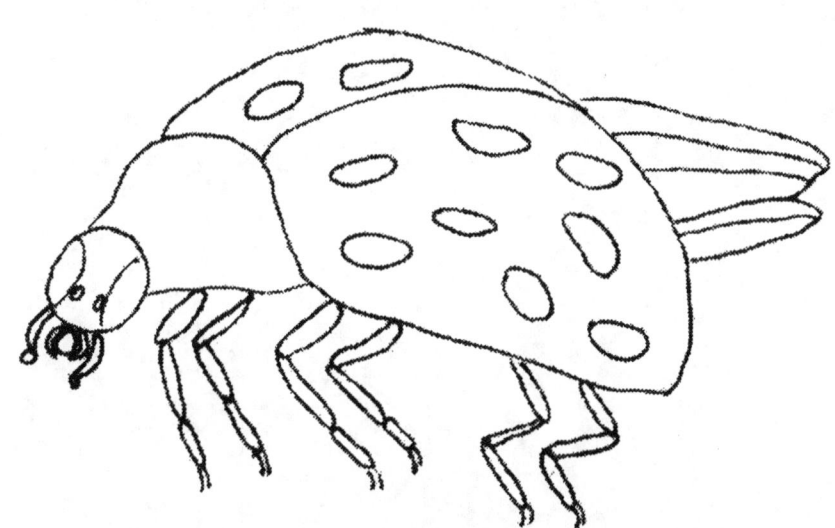

MAMMALS

Mammals, mammals
have fur or hair.
They're warm-blooded creatures
like a cat or a bear.

They give milk to their young,
and most have four legs.
Their babies come out whole
and not from eggs.

Bear

Bears come in three colors:
white, black, and brown.
They're very powerful creatures
with four paws that touch the ground.

They eat small animals,
fish, berries, and leaves.
Some even hibernate,
but not all as some believe.

I've never touched one,
not even for fun.
Unless it was a fluffy playmate
Stuffed teddy bears are really great.

Beaver

Beavers build dams and lodges,
and are hardworking creatures, we know.
They always live near water,
constantly moving to and fro.

One of the largest rodents
with flat tails and webbed feet.
They are mostly nocturnal and have big teeth,
which help them to work and eat,
and makes their day complete.

Camel

Dromedary camels have one hump,
while the Bactrian camels have two.
The desert is their typical habitat,
and they're useful to people there too.

They store fat in their humps for emergency food,
and can go without water for five days.
They have large feet that don't sink in the sand.
They really have such interesting ways.

Cat

Cats have kittens,
yes they do.
They're feline creatures,
and they're very soft too.

They meow and purr
and have different colored fur.
You can always tell
If it's a him or a her.

Cheetah

Cheetahs have strong legs
and a muscular physique.
Cheetahs are master hunters.
All sized animals are their tasty treat.

The fastest big cat,
In Africa and Asia they reside.
When a cheetah is on the prowl,
there are not many places to hide.

Cow

Cows live on farms and stay together in herds.
They love to eat grass and hay.
Cows have to be cared for by a farmer
who milks them every day.

Cows are raised for many purposes:
Milk, cheese, other dairy products, and beef.
Cows also produce leather hide for clothes and shoes.
A dairy cow's life span is very brief.

Deer

A male deer has antlers
and is called a stag or a buck.
Sometimes they fight with other males,
and they can certainly run amok.

A female deer is called a doe.
Deer eat shrubs, twigs, nuts, plants, and grass.
A baby deer is called a fawn.
Some have been know to dart onto roads as cars pass.

Dog

Bow wow, woof, woof,
and arf, arf too.
These are onomatopoeia sounds
that different dogs do.

A best friend to all
so many people say.
There are different breeds and varieties
we see every day.

Donkey

Donkeys are members of the horse family.
They both sort of look the same.
But the donkey is a work animal,
and it is very tame.

Donkeys are known by many names.
They enjoy rolling on the ground.
If you have a donkey on a farm,
it's a great animal to have around.

Elephant

The largest land mammals
so big and gray.
They have long trunks
that they use in different ways.

They're good in the circus,
and their tusks are like big teeth.
I wouldn't want an elephant
to step on my feet.

Fox

Very sly characters
in nursery rhymes.
Cunning tricksters,
time after time.

Foxes are skillful hunters
that prey on rodents, insects, and birds.
They are mostly active at night,
which is the time that they prefer.

Giraffe

The tallest mammal in the world
with a neck so long,
a big, long tongue,
and a mouth so strong.

They eat the juiciest leaves
at the tops of the trees.
They travel in groups.
I wonder if they sneeze.

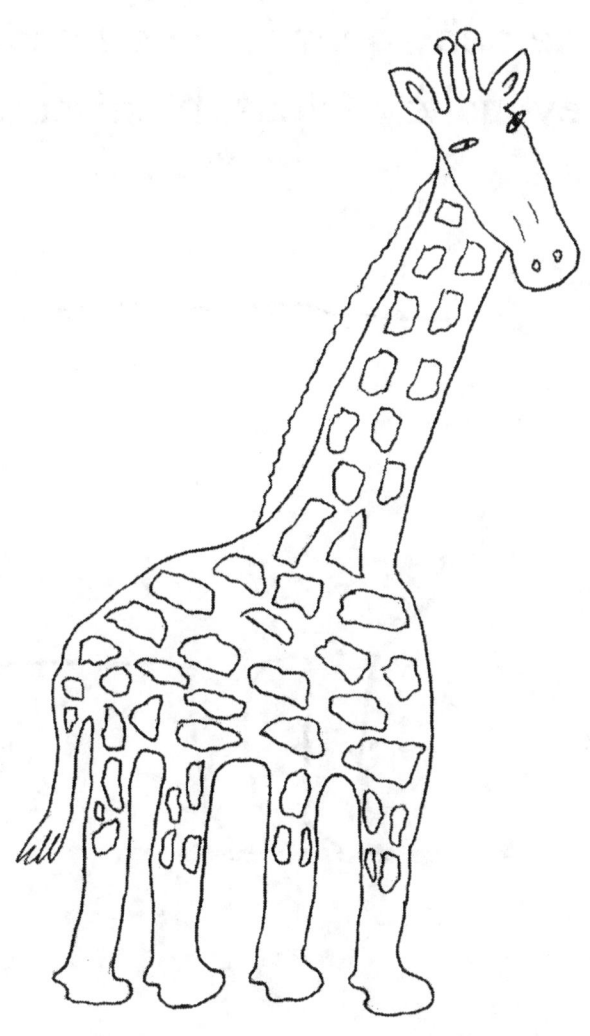

Goat

Goats live on farms and
eat grass, leaves, and twigs.
They all have to be cared for as well.
A farmer milks the nanny goat daily.
while billy goats can have a really bad smell.

Their hooves can grow very quickly.
Every month they should be cut down.
The female goat is called a nanny.
The baby goat is called a kid.
They make a bleat, bleat sound.

Hippopotamus

The enormous hippo dives and swims so well
with the help of his strong legs and webbed toes.
In ancient Greek, his name means "River Horse."
Above the water we can see his ears, eyes, and nose.

Hippos are herbivores, mostly active at night,
And boy, do they eat lots of grass!
They live in large herds, and the females are called cows.
Oh wow! Can they run fast!

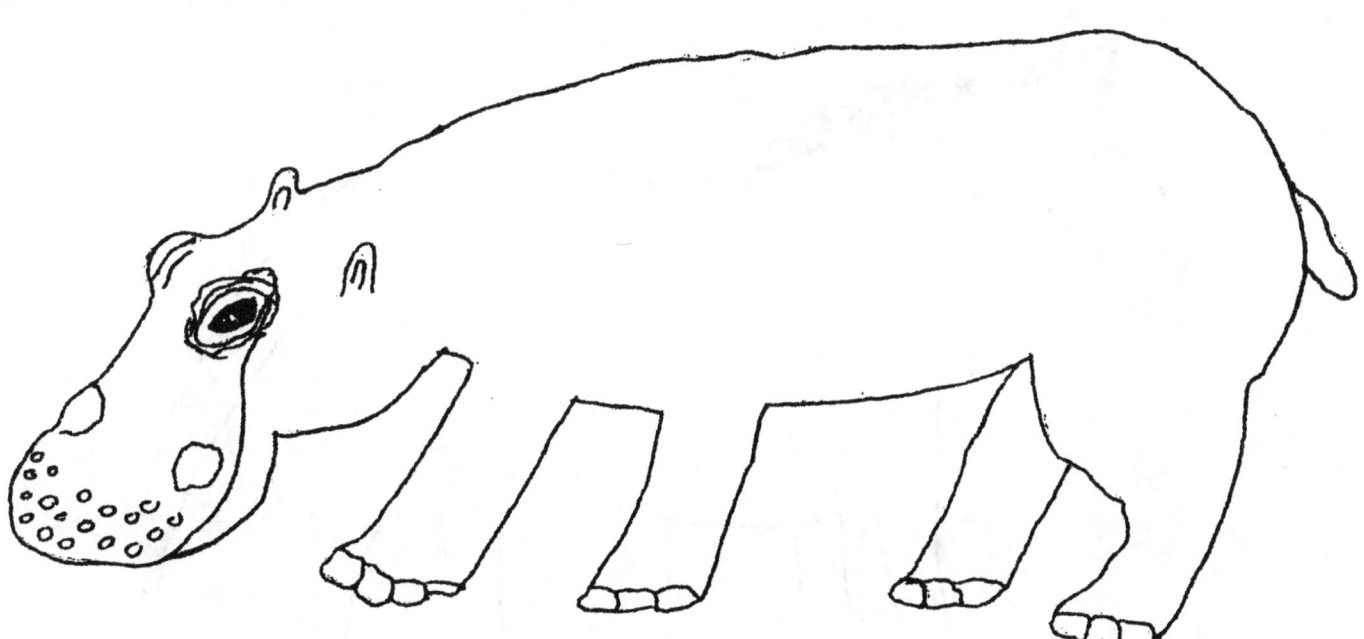

Horse

Giddy-up, giddy-up
Gallop away!
They trot very proud,
and they love to eat hay.

They're very smart animals
and easy to train.
You can steer them left or right
by using the reins.

Lion

Lions are giant cats,
the king of the pride,
the king of the jungle.
They're known far and wide.

They have a cool mane
around their head.
They have a loud roar
all the other animals dread.

Monkey

Monkey see
and monkey do.
Monkeys can do
the same as you.

They're very smart,
and they have long tails.
Some swing from trees
like in "Caps for Sale."

Ooh ooh, ahh ahh
is what they say.
They can be very funny
in so many ways.

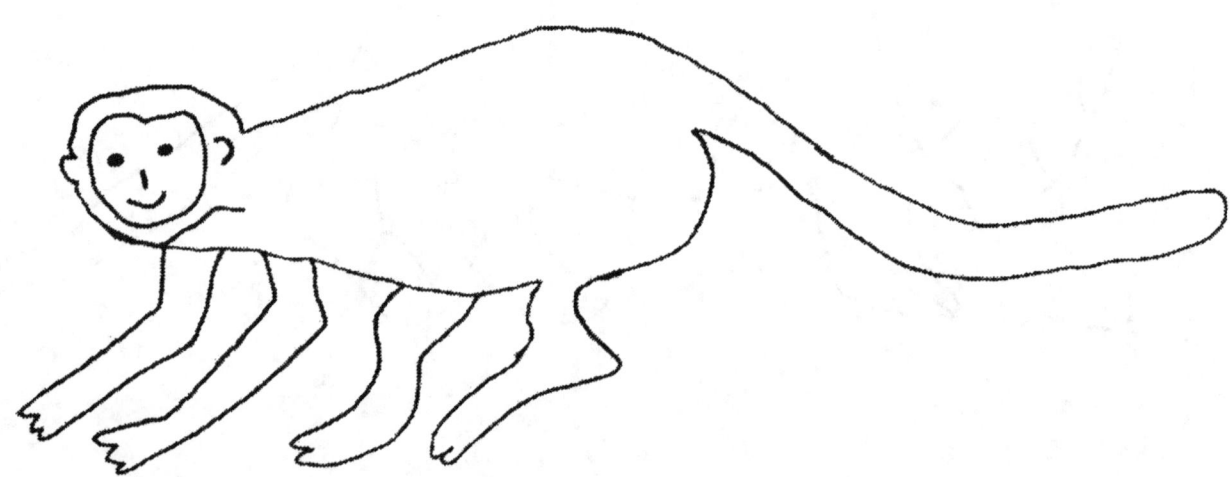

Pig

Pigs have stocky bodies, a flat snout, and small eyes.
Most are pink and have big ears.
They are also known as hogs and swine
and roll in mud to cool off, which is clear.

Pigs are raised all over the world.
They produce many products we all use:
Pork, lard, leather and glue,
fertilizer and medicines.
Now this is very good news.

Platypus

A very unusual creature.
It has a flat bill and webbed feet like a duck.
With a paddle-shaped tail like a beaver,
its appearance can leave you awestruck.

It is also a venomous mammal.
The males have venom glands in their hindfeet
and use them against predators in battle.
These features make it very unique.

Porcupine

Porcupines have pointy quills
on their neck, back, and tail,
to protect them from their enemies,
which they do without fail.

They feed on plant buds, bark, and twigs,
Such a tasty treat!
Very unique creatures
from their head to their feet.

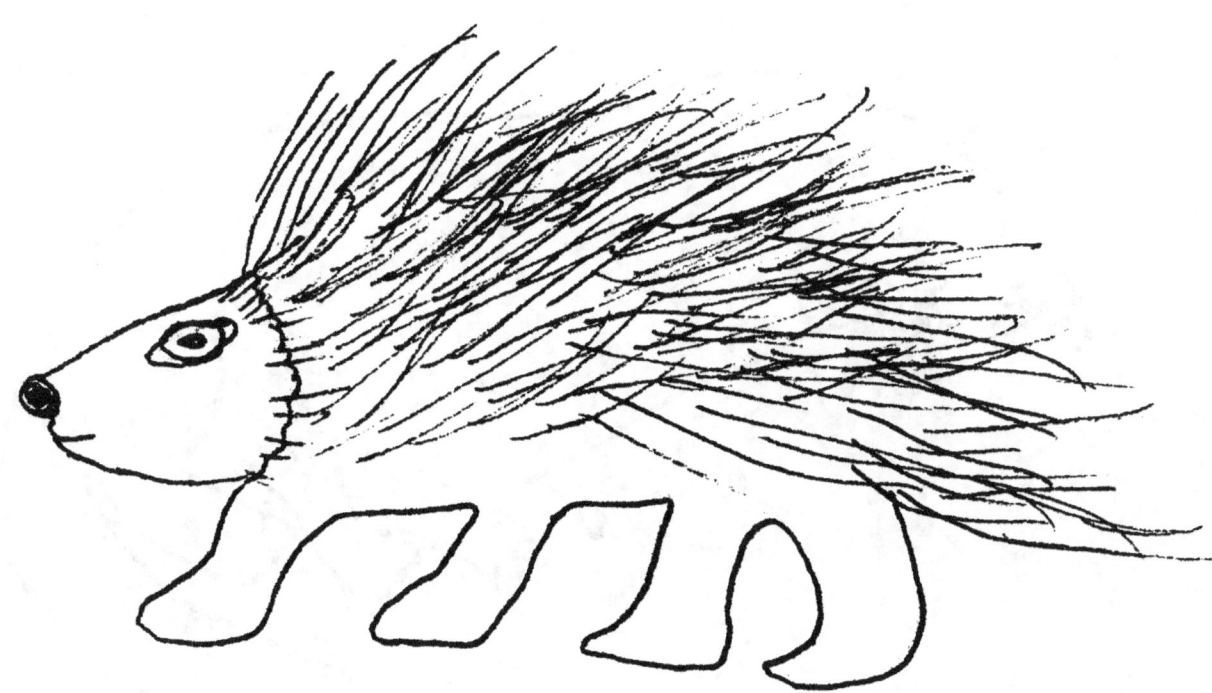

Otter

The otter is a marine mammal
that loves to swim in the sea.
They have webbed feet
and thick fur, as we can all see.

They are often seen in the water,
floating on their backs.
That's where they eat and rest
and groom themselves.
Now those are interesting facts.

Rabbit

They hop, hop, hop
with their short, little feet.
They have a cute cottontail
that's really quite unique.

They go by the name "bunny"
and also "hare."
They love to eat lettuce and carrots,
and they're very easy to scare.

Rhinoceros

Rhinos are large herbivores,
They have a distinctive horned snout.
They are an endangered species.
So, rhinos better watch out!

They use their horns to defend themselves,
but they don't have any front teeth.
They rely on their lips to pluck up plants,
so this is how they eat,
which is quite a challenging feat.

Sheep

Sheep live on farms
and stay together in flocks.
In the fields, they eat grass all day.
When it gets really cold, their wooly coats
keep them warm.
The farmer keeps them close so they don't stray.

In the summer when it gets hot,
the farmer cuts off their wool,
which doesn't hurt the sheep at all.
A sheep's coat is called fleece,
which is sold all around the world.
It's used to make clothes we buy at the mall.
I hope I can find a nice shawl.

Squirrel

Sometimes I see squirrels out my window,
scurrying from place to place.
As I walk, I might be rather close to one,
but they never ever give chase.

These rodents scurry up and down trees.
Their sharp claws help them to climb.
In fall, they gather acorns for winter
when food is hard to find.

Tiger

Orange with black stripes
as you can see.
Another cool creature
in the cat family.

He's the largest of them all
and the most powerful too.
They like to hunt at night
as many other animals do.

Whale

The largest mammal in the world
is the great blue whale.
I've heard many stories about it
and many tall, tall tales.

They're an endangered species,
not many are still here.
There are many different kinds.
Their songs are very clear.

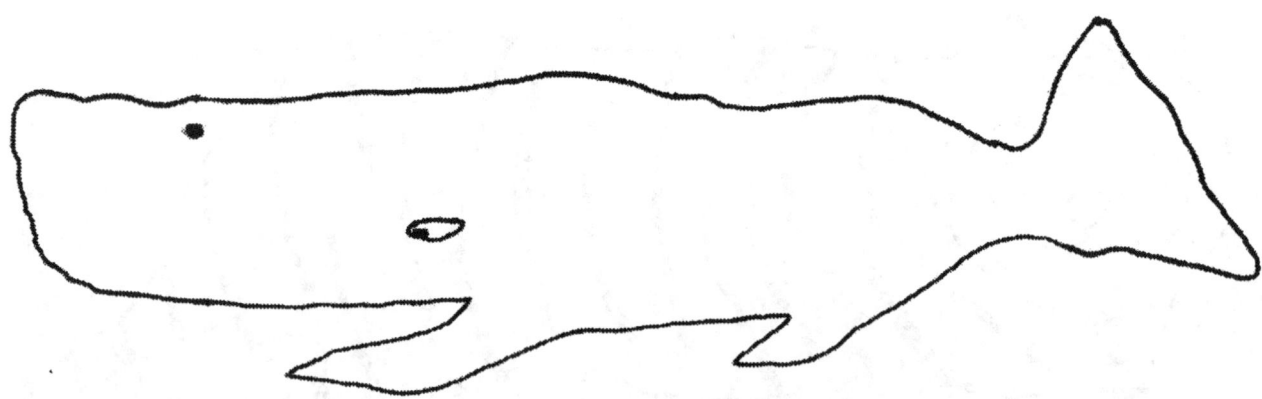

Zebra

No one know why
they're white and black
with really cool stripes
going down their backs.

They look like a horse
in a unique disguise.
They're in the same family
with a slightly smaller size.

MARSUPIALS

Marsupials are animals
with a funny name.
These animals have pouches.
Australia's their main domain.

Koalas and wallabies,
opossums and kangaroos,
all carry babies in their pouch
where they play peek-a-boo.

Kangaroo

Kangaroos, kangaroos,
hopping all around.
They can jump as high as ten feet
on their Australian Outback playground.

The baby is called a joey.
In mommy's pouch is where he stays
until he grows up big enough
or when danger goes away.

Koala

Koalas are not so cuddly and nice
as others may believe.
If you bother them, they'll give you a bite.
So please don't be deceived.

They live in small groups or all alone,
And feed on leaves from the eucalyptus tree.
Baby stays in their pouch or on their back.
They're really adorable to see.

Opossum

Opossums are good climbers
and have long, bushy tails.
They wrap them around branches
to help them climb without fail.

They feed on leaves and fruits.
Their babies stay close by.
They can also hold their baby in their pouch.
Sometimes they're a little shy.

MOLLUSKS
(AKA SOFTIES)

There's a special group of sea creatures.
They are similar but different also.
This group is called mollusks (AKA Softies).
They were discovered many years ago.

Mollusk are also called invertebrates,
which means they don't have a backbone.
They have soft, muscular bodies,
and many are pretty well known.

Octopus

An octopus can be different sizes,
It has eight long tentacles or arms.
Each arm has rows and rows of suction cups
to protect them from every kind of harm.

The arms also help them catch food.
They have a secret weapon too.
They can spew out black ink all around,
so no one can see what they do.
The water turns really dark too.
Then they can hide from you.

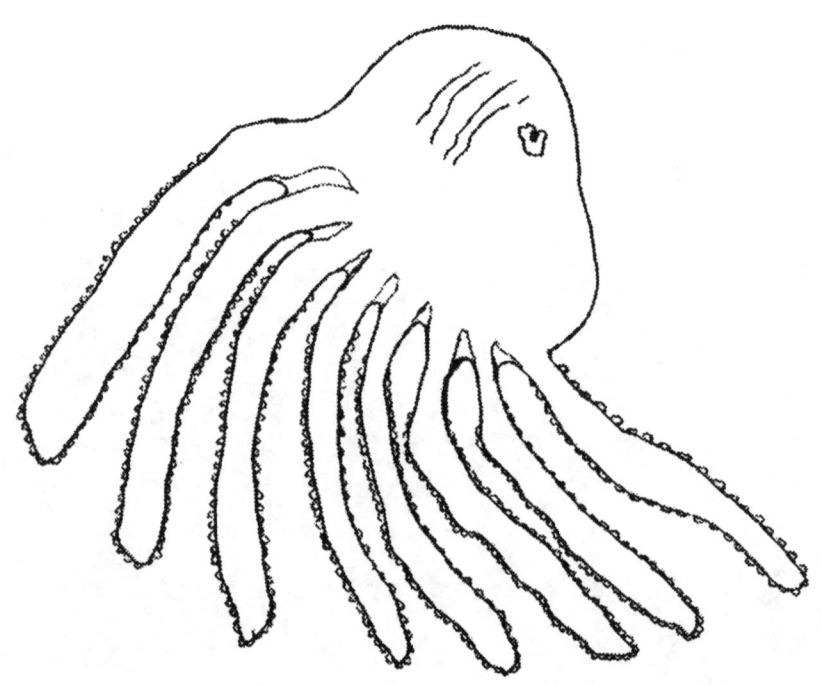

Snail

Snails have a soft body
protected by a coiled shell.
If bad weather or danger threatens,
they can hide in this home as well.

They like to eat leaves and flowers
and can live on land or in the sea.
They move very, very slowly
and leave a trail of slime so messy!

Squid

Squids can grow
big or small.
With ten tentacles around their mouth,
they swim and do not crawl.

Their tentacles are like a jellyfish
with fins like a regular fish.
They look like many different things
and can do almost whatever they wish.

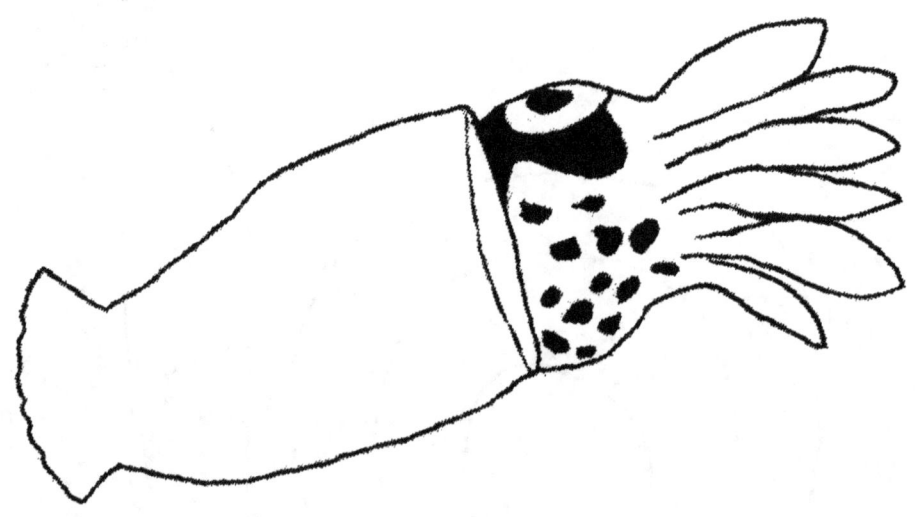

REPTILES

Reptiles can grow
so very old.
They like to bask in the sun
or so I've been told.

Cold-blooded animals,
they do lay eggs.
They have scaly or hard skin
and short, stubby legs,
except a snake.

Alligator

Alligators are sneaky predators
who lie under water and wait to catch their prey.
A fish, a turtle, or a snake,
would make them a nice dinner any day.

In winter, they dig a hole in the muddy riverbank.
In spring it awakes to find food.
Humans have hunted alligators for their skin
and used it to make bags and shoes.

Dinosaur

Dinosaurs are reptiles
from long ago.
Now they're extinct,
but they fascinate us so.

They roamed the land and swam the seas.
Some ate plants and some ate meat.
Some dinosaurs were enormous,
and some were very meek.
Yet each kind was so unique.

Lizard

Komodo dragons, geckos,
iguanas, and chameleons
are all part of a family
called reptilians.

They are really cool lizards
and unique in their own way.
Some change colors,
and they all love a nice hot day.

If their tail breaks off,
another will grow back.
Now that's no tale,
It's an amazing fact.

Snake

Slither, slither
all around.
In a tree
or on the ground.

Some are poisonous
so just beware.
If you see one around,
use lots of care
and don't try to scare.

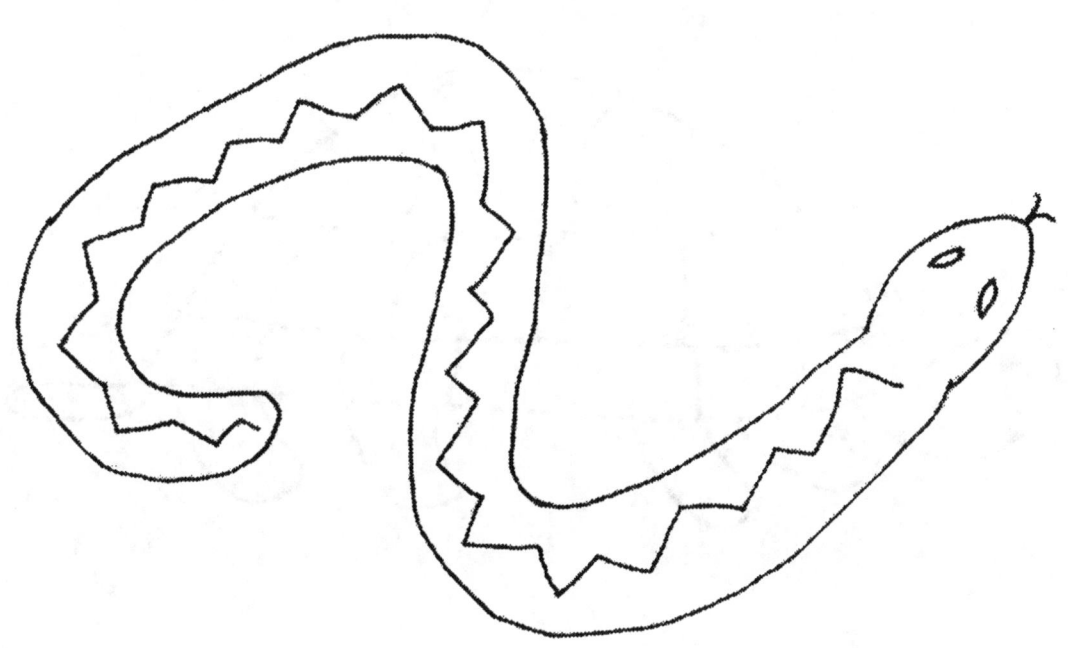

Turtle

Slow moving creatures
with such a weight on their backs.
A big, hard shell
very useful for taking naps.

It's also used for protection
when enemies are near.
They close up like a little rock
so no one can see or hear.

ANIMALS ON THE MOVE

Some animals swim in the ocean blue,
Some animals walk or crawl around,
Some animals fly up in the sky,
Some animals run or hop around.

Animals are curious creatures
that move in many different ways.
I can pretend to move just like them
and play all the games that they play.

Camouflage

Many animals
camouflage
like a hidden animal
in a forest collage.

To avoid being eaten
and avoid being seen,
Some animals change colors.
Some blend into background scenes.

Habitats

Habitats are places
where animals stay.
Cozy, cool surroundings
where they romp and play:

A forest, a desert,
A farm or the sea
A home just right
for their family.

Hibernation

Some animals go for a really long sleep
when winter rolls around.
Some animals sleep in a cozy cave
or in a hole down in the ground.

Some bears and badgers, snakes and groundhogs
take a long, sleepy, winter vacation.
They sleep until spring when the birdies sing,
and this is called hibernation.

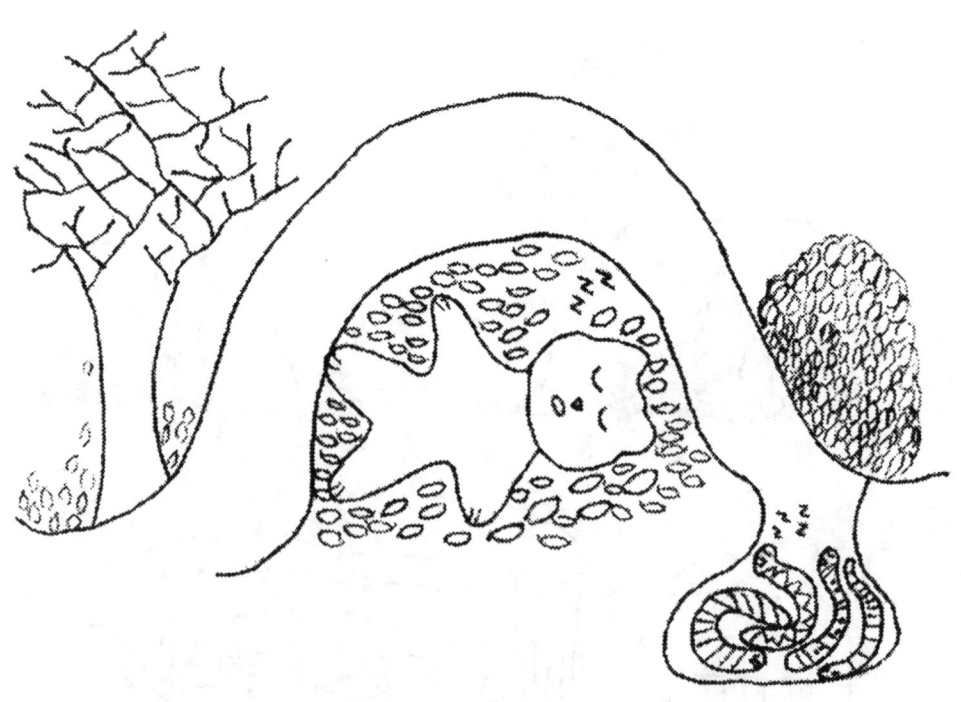

Migration

Some animals move from one place to another,
Sometimes because it's so cold.
If they can't find food,
they have to travel and move
to a place where they can be happy.

Some birds and butterflies,
whales and seals,
travel so far away.
But when the seasons change,
they travel back
to a place where they can be happy.

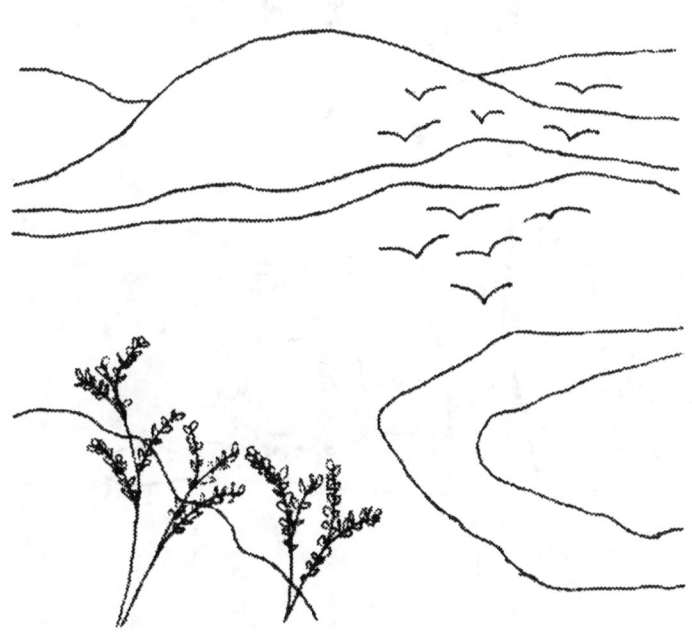

Nocturnal Animals

These animals sleep all during the day
in a cave, hole, or burrow underground.
Then when it is night, the owl takes flight,
and the aardvark looks for ants on the ground.

Bats and badgers, foxes and raccoons
prefer to look for food at dusk.
When their home is dark and gray,
night animals catch their prey,
for finding food is really a must.

About the Author

 Linda Taylor has molded kids' lives as a teacher for more than 25 years. She uses her poetry, songs, and chants in her kindergarten classroom to enhance learning and motivate her students. Linda holds an M.S. degree in Education from C.U.N.Y. at City College. She's the author of the AMAZING ANNABELLE series, which has eleven chapter books. Linda is also the author of the DARING DAVID chapter book series, which consists of 11 books. She lives with her family in Long Island, NY.

She has also authored three other poetry books:
>ALPHABET, NUMBER, AND COLOR POETRY
>POEMS THROUGHOUT THE YEAR AND BEYOND
>POETRY RHYMES FOR THE HEART, SOUL, AND MIND

www.ingramcontent.com/pod-product-compliance
Lightning Source LLC
Chambersburg PA
CBHW081753100526
44592CB00015B/2413